Jane Goodall

The Chimpanzee's Friend

Carol Fuchs

illustrated by Robin Richesson

The Rourke Corporation, Inc. Vero Beach, Florida

© 1993 by The Rourke Corporation, Inc.

All rights reserved. No part of this book may be reproduced or utilized in any form or by any means, electronic or mechanical including photocopying, recording, or by any information storage and retrieval system without permission in writing from the publisher.

The Rourke Corporation, Inc.
P.O. Box 3328, Vero Beach, FL 32964

Series Editor: Gregory Lee
Production: The Creative Spark, San Clemente, CA

Library of Congress Cataloging-in-Publication Data

Fuchs, Carol A.
    Jane Goodall - the chimpanzee's Friend / by Carol Fuchs.
       p. cm. — (Reaching your goal)
    Summary: A brief biography of the English zoologist known for her work with chimpanzees at the Gombe Stream Reserve in Tanzania. Includes information on setting goals.
    ISBN 0-86593-262-X
    1. Goodall, Jane, 1934- .—Juvenile literature. 2. Women primatologists—Biography—Juvenile literature. [1. Goodall, Jane, 1934- . 2. Zoologists. 3. Chimpanzees.] I. Title. II. Series.
QL31.G58F83 1993
591'.092—dc20
[B]
                                                                         93-6506
                                                                         CIP
                                                                          AC

Jane Goodall was a born animal lover. One night her mother Vanne looked in on her two-year-old daughter. She found Jane sleeping with earthworms under her pillow.

When Jane was just four she sat inside a chicken coop. She waited five hours for a chicken to lay an egg. "I had always wondered where on a hen was an opening big enough for an egg to come out." She found out.

Jane Goodall was born in England on April 3, 1934. Her father was an engineer and her mother a writer. When Jane was 18 months old her mother gave her a stuffed toy chimp. Jane named it Jubilee. She still has Jubilee today.

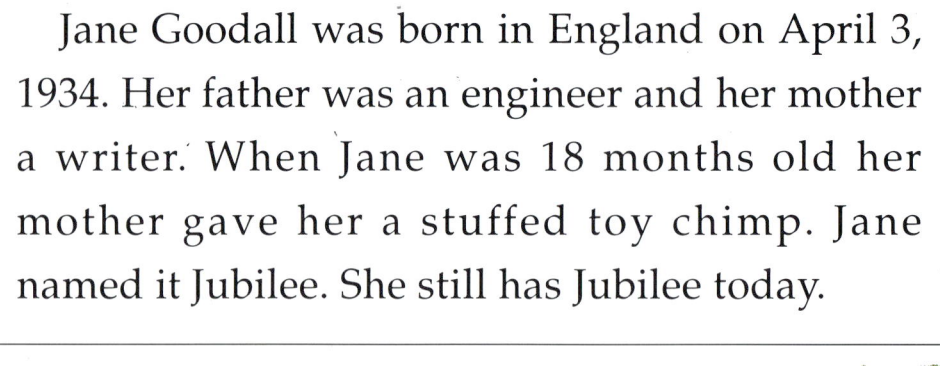

Jane loved animals and the outdoors. She could watch animals for hours. She always kept notes about the way animals behaved. Jane wanted to go to Africa one day and study them. Her teachers told her that "no girl can do that." But Jane believed in herself.

Once Jane saw a farm for old horses. The farm needed money to feed the horses. So Jane started a nature museum in her backyard. She had skulls of mice and foxes. Visitors could see birds' eggs and sea shells. They paid to see her museum. Then Jane gave the money to the horse farm.

After Jane graduated from high school she found a job. But she wanted to do something special with her life. She wanted to go to Africa. Then a friend invited Jane to her parents' farm in Kenya. Kenya is a country in East Africa. Africa at last!

Jane traveled to Nairobi where she went to see Louis Leakey. This man was a famous scientist. He believed that the first human beings lived in Africa. To prove his ideas he had to dig in the dirt to find old bones.

Leakey hired Jane. She helped him and Mrs. Leakey look for bones. "Somehow he must have sensed that my interest in animals was not just a passing phase," Jane recalled. She learned much from working with Dr. Leakey.

Dr. Leakey asked Jane if she would study the chimpanzees near Lake Tanganyika. He wanted to learn more about them. "I could hardly believe it," Jane said. "Of course I accepted."

Jane was just 24 years old. Other scientists thought Dr. Leakey was making a mistake. Jane had no experience or training. But Leakey thought those were good reasons to send Jane. He wanted someone who was open to new ideas. Jane was perfect for the job.

In 1960, Jane went to live in Gombe Stream Game Reserve. Her mother came, too. Jane remembers the day the two of them arrived. "It was a dry, beautiful day. After we set up our tents I climbed up into the hills. I met a troop of barking baboons and knew then that my dream had come true."

Jane walked into the forest every morning before dawn. She stumbled through thick bushes and climbed steep slopes to find the chimpanzees. Jane could hear them hooting and screeching far away. For two months the chimps ran away from her.

Day after day Jane watched the chimps from a distance. The chimps were not afraid of her because she was so far away. Jane saw chimps greet each other with hugs and kisses. They walked together and held hands. Jane watched them just like she watched the hen as a little girl.

Jane sometimes spent the night outdoors near the chimps to watch them sleep. They made nests for themselves out of twigs and branches. Later Jane discovered that chimps make tools. They use twigs to get termites out of termite holes. Then the chimps eat the crunchy bugs.

Jane's work amazed scientists. Chimps were not mean animals. They were smart and playful. Scientists would not have known these things by watching chimps in cages. Jane's way of studying the chimps in the wild was exciting!

"The only sure way of finding out how an animal really lives and behaves is to watch an individual or a group for very long periods of time," Jane said.

After a long time the chimps allowed Jane to play with them. They visited her tent. Her husband Hugo took many photographs and films of Jane with the chimps. These films were shown on television and made Jane famous. Now no one could doubt Jane Goodall.

In 1965, Jane earned an important degree from Cambridge University in England. She never finished college but she is now a great scientist.

Today Dr. Jane Goodall tries to help protect chimps in zoos and in the wild. "Surely we can reach out to help the chimpanzees," she said. "We must speak for them—for they cannot speak for themselves."

Jane changed the way today's scientists study animals. Her mother had told her, "if you want something you must work and fight for it. You only get something by your own efforts." Jane followed her mother's wise advice. She worked hard for her dream, and her dream came true.

Reaching Your Goal

What do you want to do? Do you want to be an astronaut? A cook? If you want something you must first set goals. Here are some steps to help you reach them.

1. **Explore Your Goals**
   Asking questions can help you decide if reaching your goal is what you really want.
   Will I be happier if I reach this goal?
   Will I be healthier if I reach this goal?

2. **Name Your Goals**
   It is harder to choose a goal if it is too general. Do you want to be "happy?"
   Learn to blow up a balloon.
   Learn to ride a two-wheel bicycle.
   Finish a book a week.

   Name the goals you want to reach.

3. Start Small
Try reaching your goal with smaller goals.
Do you want to learn to skateboard?
Try standing on it first without moving.
Do you want to build a dollhouse?
Have an adult show you how to use tools.

4. Small Goals Turn Into Big Ones
Learning to improve your spelling can be a goal.
Practice shorter words first.
Learn to use bigger words in sentences.
Enter a spelling bee.

5. Stick With It
People like Jane Goodall reached their goals by working hard. They didn't let others talk them out of their goals. You can do it too!

Reaching Your Goal Books

Jim Abbott Left-handed Wonder

Hans Christian Andersen A Fairy Tale Life

Cher Singer and Actress

Chris Burke He Overcame Down Syndrome

Henry Cisneros A Hard Working Mayor

Beverly Cleary She Makes Reading Fun

Bill Cosby Superstar

Roald Dahl Kids Love His Stories

Jane Goodall The Chimpanzee's Friend

Jim Henson Creator of the Muppets

Jesse Jackson A Rainbow Leader

Michael Jordan A Team Player

Ted Kennedy, Jr. A Lifetime of Challenges

Jackie Joyner-Kersee Track-and-Field Star

Ray Kroc Famous Restaurant Owner

Christa McAuliffe Reaching for the Stars

Dale Murphy Baseball's Gentle Giant

Charles Schulz Great Cartoonist

Arnold Schwarzenegger Hard Work Brought Success

Dr. Seuss We Love You

Samantha Smith Young Ambassador

Steven Spielberg He Makes Great Movies

The Rourke Corporation, Inc.
P.O. Box 3328
Vero Beach, FL 32964